BUSH SONG

TRICIA OKTOBER

Hodder
Children's
Books
Australia

A thousand and one tiny seeds spilled from a seed pod. Seeds, tinier than a grain of sand, were carried by the wind. They fell on black tarred roads, grey cement and red roofs. Some came to rest on dry dusty dirt and some on hard yellow rocks. None of these would have a chance to grow.

One tiny seed fell on a sad and ugly place where all the trees were gone. The earth was warm and brown and still remembered the forest that had grown, not long ago, tall and green above her. She remembered when the roots of the trees held her tight and the wind couldn't blow her away.

The earth longed for the trees again and fed and cared for the tiny seed. It was the beginning of a tree.

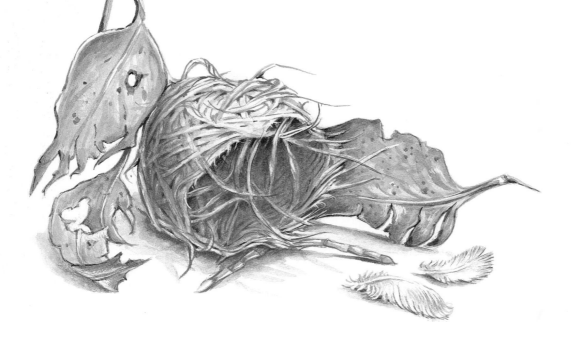

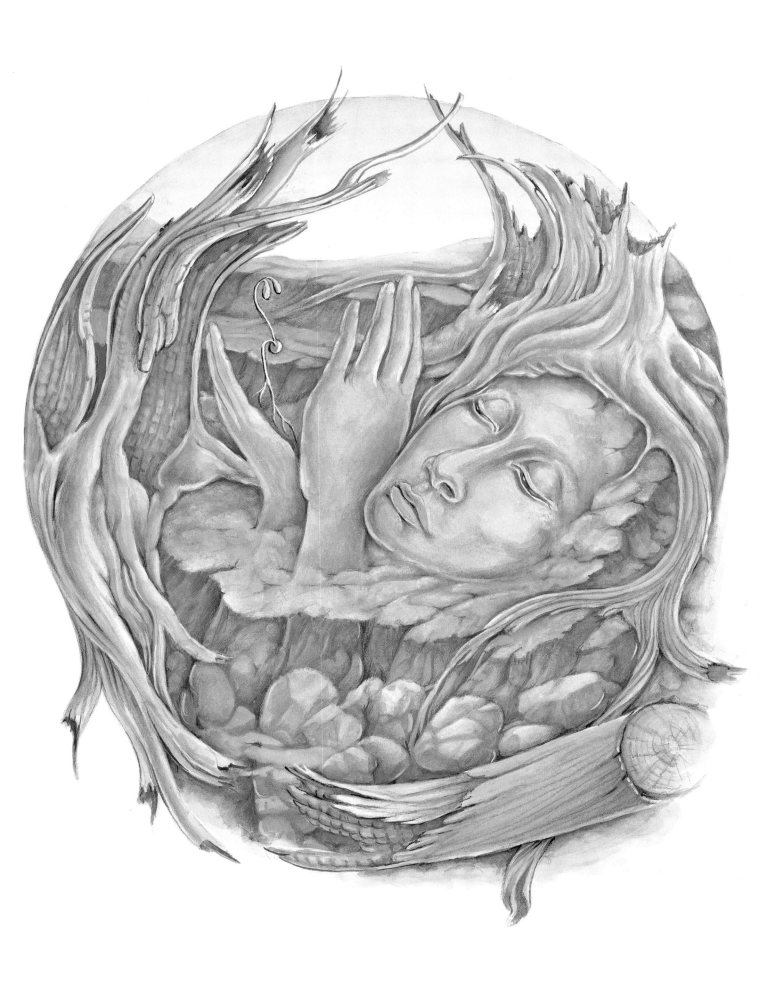

The seedling grew up tall and straight, towards the sun. The seeds of other plants also came to rest on the earth and many of them grew. Soon coarse weeds and blackberries were everywhere, growing around the little tree and choking out delicate plants.

The tree grew taller and the branches spread wider. The leaves on the tree became thicker until there was not enough sun in its shade for the blackberries to grow.

The tree kept growing tall and wide and shady. Birds visited the tree to rest a while and sing, but they didn't stay. Butterflies fluttered about, and drifted off.

The tree kept growing — tall and wide and shady. But one tree isn't the same as a forest of trees and the earth still longed for a forest. Cicadas came and screamed loud love songs to one another. They stayed.

The tree grew bigger and made buds.

The tree kept growing up towards the sun.

Little lizards came and hid under the dry leaves that had fallen to the ground.

The tree was big now, but still it kept growing — tall and wide and shady.

Red ants arrived and made nests near the roots and small mushrooms grew in the tree's shade.

Huntsman spiders made their homes under the loose bark on the tree trunk.

The buds on the tree swelled and burst open. Soon fluffy white gum blossoms covered the branches.

Native bees, little, black and stingless, smelt the pollen on the blossoms and came to feed. They stayed.

Many insects were enticed by the sweet honey smell of the nectar. Feral honey bees came but they didn't stay.

Beetles came and small grey tree frogs. They both stayed.

A possum smelt the blossom and came to eat at night, but she didn't stay. One tree isn't a forest and only in a forest is a small possum safe.

The gumnuts ripened and a thousand and one tiny seeds spilled out and were carried by the wind. Some came to rest on the warm brown earth and they grew.

The earth remembered the tall green forest as the seedling roots went deep and held her tight against the wind and rain.

But it was only the beginning of a forest. Hungry caterpillars can be the death of a small tree. So too can the rabbits living under the blackberry roots. A small tree growing up towards the sun can make a tasty meal for a rabbit.

Not all the seeds that grew lived long enough to become trees. But some did.

Two scarlet robins came and built a nest of dry grass bound with cobwebs. They lined it with feathers and plant-down and decorated the outside with moss and lichen. The nest was a crib for three pale green eggs speckled with brown. The robins felt safe and sheltered, hidden amongst the leaves of the big tree.

Other birds came and built their nests and raised their babies.

The big tree grew still bigger. Each year the branches were full of blossom, then gumnuts and finally thousands of tiny seeds were spilling into the wind trying to find a place to grow. Gradually little trees began to fill the empty spaces and small creatures felt safe enough to come and live there.

The young trees grew taller, their branches became wider and their leaves thicker, until there was not enough sun for the blackberries and weeds to grow anywhere. Now there was just enough sun for delicate ferns and dainty ground-orchids to grow.

The possum came back to eat the nectar from the gum blossoms and stayed. A family of feathertail gliders came. They built a nest of dried gum leaves where they spent the daytime, all curled up together. At night they fed on nectar and chased moths and insects from one tree to another.

All the trees kept growing.

They dropped their old leaves and each year shed their bark. Soon a thick carpet of compost covered the earth making it rich and fertile. From the wind-scattered seeds more plants grew. More animals came and the lyre bird built a stage to dance on.

In the big tree some of the old branches became grey and hollow. Fairy owls found the hollows and made their nests. Tiny bats slept upside down in the hollows not used by the owls.

At last a forest again stood tall and green above the warm brown earth.

A forest for all the animals and insects, flowers and ferns.

A place for frogs and birds and lizards to live in.

Never again would all the trees be destroyed.

Now enough people cared and they taught their children to care about the forests.

The voices of all the creatures rose loud and clear as they sang the bush song.

A song of sounds.

The wind made music in the leaves and a thousand and one tiny seeds burst from a seed-pod.

The forest could now stand tall and green and safe for ever.

Notes on illustrations:

P. 2 Gumnuts and leaves of lemon-scented gum (*Eucalyptus citriodora*). This eucalypt has lemon-scented leaves; it grows to a height of forty metres with a spread of four metres and the seed-pods (gumnuts) are typical of eucalypts. Qld and NSW.

Pp. 4 & 5 Land cleared for farming has left many native plants and animals without suitable habitats so they have become extinct. Those remaining are in even greater danger from wood-chipping and logging in forests and the spread of towns.

P. 6 Caterpillar of the monarch or wanderer butterfly (*Danaus plexippus*) feeding on milkweed (*Asclepias*). Milkweed was introduced to Australia from America and Africa and has become a noxious weed.

P. 7 The European blackberry (*Rubus fruticosus*) has also become a noxious weed. Its long stems take root wherever they touch the ground and the seeds are spread by birds and animals.
Sparrows, introduced from Europe and Asia, a nuisance because they compete with native birds for food and nesting sites; the common garden snail, also introduced to Australia.
Long-necked mantis (*Pseudomantis albofiniata*).

P. 8 Jezebel butterfly (*Delias aganippe*). The larvae feed on mistletoe which attaches itself to trees like this eucalypt. Qld, NSW, Vic., SA.
P. 9 The orchard butterfly (*Papilio aegeus aegeus*). The larvae feed on citrus leaves and other plants and its range extends as new citrus orchards are planted. Qld, NSW, Vic., SA.
Silvereye (*Zosterops lateralis*). Found in all states of Australia, this little bird eats fruit and nectar and the male has a rich warbling song. Cicada (*Cyclochilla australasiae*). This one is a 'Green Monday'.

P. 10 Tree fungi (*Polyporus*) grow in colonies on wood and can live for several years; small common blue butterfly (*Erina hyacinthina hyacintha*). Widespread.
P. 11 Common skink (*Lampropholis guichenoti*).
When not sunning themselves, to be found amongst foliage on dry ground; female lays 2 or 3 eggs under stones or bark. Widespread.

P. 12 Cow-boy beetle (*Diaphonia dorsalis*). Feeds on flowers and nectar; egg-case of praying mantis; bag-moth case.
P. 13 Peron's tree frog (*Litoria peronii*) widespread; common small green mantis (*Orthodera ministralis*) widespread; skipper butterfly (fam. *Hesperiidae*) found throughout Australia.
Christmas beetles (*Anoplognathus* species); orb-weaving spider (genus *Araneus*); native bees (order *Hymenoptera*) found throughout Australia; honey bees (*Apis mellifera*) introduced, gone wild, and now competing with smaller native bees.

P. 14 Emperor gum moth (*Antheraea eucalypti*) and caterpillar. East coast NSW-Vic.
P. 15 Brushtail possum (*Trichosurus vulpecula*).
The most common of all Australian possums; considerable variation in size and colour; eats leaves, particularly eucalyptus, buds, fruits, flowers and nectar. Widespread.

P. 16 Macleay's swallowtail butterfly (*Graphium macleayanus macleayanus*). Coastland from north Qld to southern Tas.

P. 18 Mole cricket (*Gryllotalpa nitidula*); long-horned grasshopper (fam. *Tettigonioidea*).
P. 19 Processionary caterpillars, the larvae of a small brown moth (*Ochrogaster contraria*). They feed at night and return to a communal nest at ground level for the day. Rabbits (*Oryctoclagus cuniculus*). Introduced and firmly established across southern Australia; now slowly spreading into Queensland.

P. 20 Superb fairy wren and nestlings (*Malurus cyaneus*), one of Australia's best-known birds. Both male and female feed the nestlings and young birds from an earlier brood often help; pretty reeling song. Qld, south to Tas. and west into SA.
P. 21 Scarlet Robin (*Petroica multicolor*). Eats mainly insects; has a modest but agreeable trilling song; often called Robin Redbreast. Qld, NSW, Vic., SA, Tas.

P. 22 Pink fingers orchid (*Caladenia carnea*).
East coast of mainland. Stone gecko or wood adder (*Diplodactylus vittatus*); grows to no more than 7 or 8 cms; found under stones and logs on moist soil, throughout Australia except Tasmania; harmless but is often killed because of its name.
P. 23 Marsupial mouse, yellow-footed Antechinus (*Antechinus flavipes*). One of the few small marsupials still seen in gardens; it feeds on insects, flowers and nectar. Widespread from Qld to south-western WA in a variety of habitats.
Pink hyacinth orchid (*Dipodium punctatum*) all states except WA; small greenhood orchid (*Pterostylus nana*).

Pp. 24 & 25 Feathertail glider/flying mouse (*Acrobates pygmaeus*). The feathertail is found right down the east coast of the mainland and inland to the drier forests and woodland. Like the gecko, it has pads on its toes, enabling it to cling to smooth surfaces.

P. 26 Nodding greenhood orchid (*Pterostylis nutans*).
Common dunnart, marsupial mouse (*Sminthopsis murina*). Eats beetles, roaches and spiders and is found in woodland in Qld, NSW, Vic., SA and WA.
P. 27 The superb lyrebird (*Menura novaehollandiae*) lives in damp gullies of forests in south-east Australia. The male spreads his beautiful tail feathers when he performs his courtship dance.

P. 28 Little broad-nosed bat (*Nycticeius greyii*). Begins to forage at dusk and often been seen taking a drink as it skims across still water. All over Australia except in Tas. and the Cape York peninsula.
P. 29 Little forest bat (*Eptesicus vulturnus*).
This tiny bat eats insects and roosts in tree hollows, sometimes shared with possums. Southern Australia including Tas.
Australian owlet/nightjar (*Aegotheles cristatus*).
Begins to hunt at dusk; lives on insects, mainly moths and beetles; found throughout Australia and including Tas. in forestlands generally.
Botany Bay Weevil (*Chrysolophus spectabilis*), the most beautifully coloured of all Australian weevils.

P. 30 Blue spotted orchid (*Thelmytira ixioides*) found in heathlands and forests, all states.
P. 31 Wonga vine (*Pandorea pandorana*) flowers spring and summer, east coast.
Evening brown butterfly (*Melanitis leda banksi*) unlike most butterflies prefers to fly at dusk and at dawn.
Green tree frog (*Litoria caerulea*). One of the most common tree frogs. Widespread along coast and inland in Qld, NSW, SA, WA, NT.
King parrot (*Alisterus scapularis*). Well known coastal species of great beauty; it nests, like many of our parrots in a hollowed eucalypt branch.